mixed media &
found materials

mixed media &
found materials

Lucy Renshaw

A & C Black ■ London

First published in Great Britain in 2009
A & C Black Publishers Limited
36 Soho Square
London W1D 3QY
www.acblack.com

ISBN: 978-1-408-10103-2

Book design: Susan McIntyre
Cover design: Sutchinda Rangsi Thompson
Commissioning Editor: Susan James
Managing Editor: Sophie Page
Copyeditor: Jo Waters
Proofreader: Julian Beecroft

Typeset in 10 on 13pt Myriad Light
Printed and bound in China

This book is produced using paper that is made from wood grown in managed, sustainable forests. It is natural, renewable and recyclable. The logging and manufacturing processes conform to the environmental regulations of the country of origin.

Disclaimer: Information given in this book is to the author's best knowledge and every effort has been made to ensure accuracy and safety but neither the author nor publisher can be held responsible for any resulting injury, damage or loss to either persons or property. Any further information which will assist in updating of any future editions would be gratefully received.

contents

acknowledgements

I would like to take this opportunity to say how hugely grateful I am to all of my family for encouraging me to write this book and supporting me through the pursuit of my career – setting up shows, help with funding, travelling all over and being my biggest fans! Special thanks to Mum for always reminding me to live my dream and never give up – don't worry Mum, I won't! Thanks to Angie for all your support and encouragement over the years, Dad for your constant ongoing help, time, energy and for generally being fantastic (and a great technician)! Finally, a big thank you to Ant for all your ideas, patience and constant positive encouragement, and for putting up with me constantly talking about it all.

I'd also like to acknowledge Arts Council England for supporting 'Maison et objet' in Paris – thank you.

introduction

Mixed Media and Found Materials guides you through lots of fun, exciting and cheap ideas to help you create your own individual designs for the interior.

In this book I aim to demonstrate how ordinary everyday items can be given a new lease of life, whilst at the same time retaining a sense of the history associated with them.

The book is about creating fabrics and ideas which can be used in many ways, not just simply transforming an old chair or cushion. We need to remember that there is nothing new about recycling, and we have many lessons to learn from our grandparents that could be applied to our throwaway society.

From an early age I have always loved to collect and use things I've found – from collecting shells and driftwood on the beach to improvising with old clothes and making teddy-bear clothes from scrap material – and I've always had a passion for arts and crafts such as papermaking, quilling, jewellery-making and fabric-printing. As a family we grew up recycling, regularly going to car-boot and jumble sales, where we'd always buy more than we sold. Our house was full of mix'n'match furniture and bric-a-brac.

In the studio

My passion for art continued through school and eventually I went on to study for a Master's Degree in Mixed Media Textiles at the Royal College of Art in London, where I specialised in interior products and textiles using found materials.

I hope this book inspires you, not only to produce new items for your home but also to think differently and more creatively about the way you work and the materials you decide to use.

There is much emphasis on spontaneous use of materials and the way ideas can be transferred, and much of what we see is based on very simple ideas which have been revisited.

Often people believe they have to pay for pieces which are considered to be 'arty' or 'trendy', but you can produce similar effects at a fraction of the cost and you will find many ideas in this book to help you achieve this.

1 why use found materials?

'Found materials' is another term for anything that has been discarded, finished with or thrown away. We will explore how to use these materials when designing textiles, which, depending on the materials, can be used to create interior products, revamp fashion garments, or create samples to frame or keep as inspiration for other projects.

There is nothing new in working with found fabrics, as particularly in times of austerity our parents and grandparents have reused everything in a spirit of 'make do and mend'. This has included taking buttons and collars off shirts, darning old socks, using the rag and bone man and returning clothing by weight in return for money. During the war years this was driven by necessity, and a busy cottage industry thrived by producing patchwork quilts made from scraps, and rag-rug floor mats, while crafts such as knitting and crochet flourished. It was only during the postwar years that our consumer society took off and we began to forget our frugal roots.

Over the last ten years or so, we have come almost full circle, with environmental concerns about global warming, our carbon footprint, pollution and conservation. We now have a situation where there is a charity shop on every corner.

Working with found materials creates at least three benefits:

- you can create something truly unique
- it helps the environment
- it contributes to charity.

In a nutshell, we've moved from necessity-driven recycling to worldwide and local political initiatives in developed countries aimed at conserving and 'saving the planet'.

Having said this, people in developing countries, from the favelas of South America to the shanty towns of Africa, still continue to recycle out of necessity. The behaviour of millions in such circumstances is characterised by foraging for and regenerating used and discarded goods. Even in this day and age you can still see young children rummaging through rubbish dumps for scrap metal to sell, or making well-crafted footwear from such things as old tyres.

The purpose of this book is to combine the aesthetic with the practical, whilst still respecting environmental issues. In some ways this is a luxury which we can all afford, but the pleasure in the finished product is heightened by knowing that you have produced a beautiful piece of work for next to nothing. You have given a new lease of life to an 'unwanted something'. Surely this must bring greater satisfaction than off-the-peg, off-the-shelf consumerism. It's as much aesthetic as eco!

2 becoming inspired

I take photos wherever I go. I personally like capturing images of close-ups and detail. Textures, patterns and colours really inspire the way I work and the ideas I come up with. I have a macro lens for my camera, but if you don't have one, and this is the way you want to work, any camera that can focus or 'zoom' can create great shots and capture details and ideas. For example, I find run-down buildings or old boats with worn colours are an interesting starting point for textiles as there are so many textures and colours to work with.

Other inspiration can come from flowers, markets, junk shops and more often than not simply in the materials I find.

I often take an image with me when I'm on my hunt for materials, which means I can look for exact colours that could be used to recreate the textures and patterns. This image (opposite) which I've taken of a long-tail boat in Thailand is a great inspiration, given the range of colours, textures and ideas that I can recreate using textile techniques.

Spirit tree, Thailand

Long-tail boat, Thailand

LEFT Vibrant flowers hang from a long-tail boat; RIGHT Inspiration photo with collected fabric

Here you can see I've collected fabrics and materials that match and complement it to create the look.

There are many ways of translating your inspiration into end-products, some of which I will discuss in the techniques chapter. For instance, create flowers similar to those on this boat to sew onto an extravagant skirt, or recreate the worn paint look on the leg of a chair.

Travel in particular inspires me, but ideas and interesting imagery are all around and right on your doorstep if you know what to look for.

Just taking a walk through a forest in autumn provides a huge range of textures and colours to look at: russet, gold-brown, green, orange, crimson – a totally natural and harmonious palette. Complete inspiration! Look hard enough and you will find these colours and textures in any number of our sources.

I find that photographing the things you like allows you to narrow down ideas. Use the viewfinder of your camera to home in on a section you like, and focus closely on particular colours, patterns and textures.

If photography is not your thing, use images from magazines, old wallpaper, pictures and articles you've collected. I keep hundreds of collected images in shoeboxes to look back on and use whenever I need new ideas. Alternatively, you can just use your found materials, fabrics, textiles and collected objects as the source of inspiration, working with existing patterns, cutting out, layering and working on top with stitch; or collage ideas using old magazine cuttings, cutting out flowers and shapes from fabrics and working with these to create finished textiles.

LEFT Colour inspiration – spices in Marrakesh; *RIGHT* Pattern inspiration – Marrakesh

Bamboo – pattern ideas

3 materials

One thing's for sure, if you use found recycled and scrap materials, not only will you create something truly unique and save money, but you will also be doing your bit to help the environment. When you're searching for unusual crafty bits and bobs, you will find everything you need plus more exciting mediums to work with. You never know what you will find, and often finding new things to work with is a great boost to creativity. I find it far more inspiring rooting around a charity shop than walking round a clean-cut craft shop where everything is in its place and costs a fortune. At a jumble sale or charity shop you have to be creative from the word go, deciding what colours and patterns go together – you will discover that some unusual things work together purely by chance. The joy of this is that you can often end up creating something that no one else can reproduce in quite the same way.

This chapter explores a range of different materials that you may encounter when searching for found materials. You will be able to refer back to this from the techniques section when choosing materials to work with. Use it only as a guide, as when you go on your own hunt you will find your own individual and special collection of materials.

Cottons/polyester

There will be an abundance of these types of fabrics in charity shops, jumble sales, etc. – anything from curtains to PJs, shirts and skirts. Mix and match the checks, stripes and patterns to create a range of designs. Pick up a selection and hold the different patterns next to one another to see what works together. Try and forget the garment, and just think about the fabric and pattern.

Knits/wool

When first looking for knitted materials you will find a lot of cardigans, jumpers, hats and scarves, most of which will be a funny shape or a huge size; just think about the colours and texture of the wool, and focus on how they complement each other. If you like it, pick it up and play around with it, place it next to other fabrics and materials, and get a feel for what works well together. You can almost create a viewfinder with your hands, to concentrate on the fabric not the garment and so imagine it in other forms.

FACING PAGE *Collection of found materials*

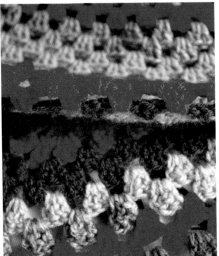

LEFT Old blanket; RIGHT Charity-shop shirts

Leather

Again there will be many leather items wherever you look. These will include old shoes, bags and coats. Of course, some will be too good to cut up, but maybe then you'll just buy it to wear, and save a few pounds on that new winter coat. It's amazing what good-quality clothes people give away. Look out for scrap leather, or really old clothes which are wearing out.

Tights and underwear!

An odd material I know, but I'm sure all of you have holey or laddered tights which normally just get thrown in the bin. However, tights make a versatile fabric as they are stretchy and come in all colours and thicknesses. I save all my old tights and use them for different techniques. Underwear on the other hand may be taking the recycling thing too far, but I like to find a use for any old scraps. Often bras and knickers have delicate lace and detailed fabrics; why not cut them up and make use of them using ideas from the following chapters? I have been known to make detailed 3D flowers from the bright-coloured lace of old (clean!) knickers – though you may want to use your own rather than someone else's!

Beads/buttons/sequins

There are many different ways to collect these kinds of materials. Sometimes charity shops have a section especially for this, but you should also look for old necklaces to cut up, buttons of shirts, sequins on old tops which you can cut up and reuse, old brooches – the list goes on. You will often come across old lampshades that have interesting tassels, and beads which can be reused to recreate a different decorative lampshade, or to redesign a totally different fashion item.

 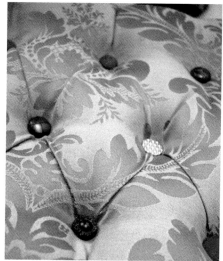

LEFT Collected beads and broken jewellery; RIGHT Stool with buttons

Denim

You will find an abundance of different denims whenever looking for old fabrics – mainly in the form of jeans, bags, hats and jackets – and in many shades and colours. If you are thinking of making something hard wearing and strong, denim would be a good material to use. You will come across odd shapes, and some dodgy clothing from the 80s, but again just think about the material.

Bric-a-brac

I often collect things that I like the look of, and then decide what I'll do with them later. You will come across an amazing assortment of bric-a-brac when sourcing a project, ranging from unusual cutlery to old clothes pegs and old bits of crockery. I have been given big jam jars full of old buttons and they always come in handy for something. Here I've re-upholstered a stool using a range of odd buttons which I gathered from old chairs. You may decide to use them on something you create later, or you may just keep them as unusual trinkets for your house. Keep them as part of your resources to generate ideas. I follow this concept so that's why my house is full of junk and hoarded stuff!

Furniture and accessories

Car-boot sales, jumble sales and looking round the tip stimulate the imagination with a huge selection of bits and pieces in lots of shapes and sizes – plates, bowls, lampshades, chairs, tables, picture frames, stools and garden goods to name just a few. I look out for unusual-shaped objects, again forgetting the pattern or colour, as these are things which will be covered when the items are redesigned.

I always leave the tip with at least something I've rescued, and normally end up going home with a van full! This practise isn't approved of by all councils however, so please check with your local council about rules and regulations.

4 sources & inspiration

Inspiration for designing is everywhere; we're surrounded by it in many different forms, shapes, colours, sizes and dimensions.

Ideas are born out of the most seemingly ordinary objects. The sources of these are infinite and it's because of this abundance that such creative, exciting and unique products come into being. For every item discarded there could be one hundred new interpretations.

A recycled object may well have a fascinating history and a sense and feel of earlier and later use. Better then to build on something old than always to buy new.

Sources include: jumble sales, car-boot sales, charity shops, scrapstores, refuse, house clearance, auctions, hand-me-downs, shop waste, grandparents and, my preferred source, skips and tips! Some tips have sections of waste which you can help yourself to, or if you have your eye on something they normally don't mind getting it for you.

Always ask friends for their old clothes and materials rather than allowing them to be thrown away. Once people know what you are up to, they will happily donate you their old goods.

Auction bargains

A junkyard

My mother runs a bag-making business (www.jumblebaggers.co.uk) where the bags are all created using reclaimed textiles. They put leaflets around the local area asking for donated fabrics, and they have bags of material left on the doorstep for reuse every day! This may be a bit extreme if you only want to make one cushion, but it's a good idea if you're thinking of mass production. It's amazing what people will throw out or donate.

5 techniques

There are many techniques we can explore when working with fabric and mixed materials, and in this section we will cover a range of simple approaches.

The ideas are very much experimental. I've never been one for following rules or instruction manuals, as I feel trial and error is the best way! The ideas may well embrace more than one technique, as this will often be dictated by the type of material or vice versa. For example, there is no obvious approach when revamping an old cushion, as you could use a range of techniques such as appliqué, pleating or hand embroidery. This section of the book includes techniques which ultimately can be used in most projects, from re-covering an old chair seat to creating your own unique design on an old skirt. The chapter is broken down into the following explanatory sections.

Tools and equipment
Some of the tools you will need.

Appliqué
Using a combination of standard and individual terminology. I particularly focus on the application and use of a material called Bondaweb.

Plaiting and cording
Making useful ropes, strings and cords from lengths of fabric.

Couching
Using cording to create patterns and textures mixed with stitch.

Wrapping
Working with fabrics to cover other materials, a good use for furniture and jewellery.

Fabric flowers
Making 3D flowers from scraps of fabric.

Raffia and ribbon shapes
Create designs with freehand stitch, using raffia and ribbon.

FACING PAGE Pegs and flowers

Scrap fabric snake draft excluders
A great way to use up any old bulky fabrics such as curtains and blankets.

Covering found objects
Working with found objects to make something unique by covering with materials.

Reusing old rags
Making the most of any old fabric you find, however old and drab.

Fabric pompoms
Creating traditional pompoms using recycled textiles.

Lazertran™
Working with a transfer-technique paper, and using it on varied materials.

Cords and flowers

Pleating
Folding, pressing and manipulating materials.

Slashing and layering
Scissor cutting and tearing through layers of fabric to expose pattern and texture.

Tools and equipment

Whatever your equipment, it must be well maintained, while scissors, knives and needles should be kept sharp and dry, and a well stocked toolbox will definitely come in handy.

Tools and equipment should always be simple, safe and cheap. Complicated methods or expensive, specialised craft materials are not normally necessary unless goods are being mass-manufactured. This book is all about making things with what you have or find, and creating them using inexpensive materials.

Below is a list of the basic range of tools and equipment I regularly use and which are most useful in my design-and-make process.

Sewing machine

I hope what I'm about to write is refreshing news for the reader! I've never been one for intricate pieces of equipment, or lengthy instruction manuals. Therefore I recommend a very simple-to-use sewing machine which does the basics. You can use lots of other stitches and techniques if you desire, but I concentrate only on using the straightforward methods, as I believe uncomplicated is best. The techniques I write about are more about the use and interpretation of materials and objects rather than complicated ways of working.

In the past I have experimented with many embroidery techniques and worked with different stitches, but in the following sections we will just be using the zigzag and straight stitches – simple but effective! If you want to go for real intricacy or detail (for example, if you need to do something more embroidery-based), there are many technical books and instructions for sewing which you can find in the library or any bookshop. If you have no interest in instruction manuals or technical procedures, take heart, as there are many straightforward ways to be creative.

When buying a sewing machine, make sure you get good after-sales support, help and guidance. A good sewing-machine shop will supply some training and sewing tips. It is for this reason that I bought mine from a shop rather than over the internet.

I recommend a machine that can sew through thick fabrics such as leather, and multiple layered fabrics. I personally only ever use the simple settings, but if you have a more complicated machine and you want to become more adventurous, you can experiment. It's best to choose a machine that allows you to do both. I have a Pfaff machine because it is hard-wearing and works well on thick fabrics, and it's very simple to use.

Some technical descriptions for your sewing machine:

Stitch type
Straight and zigzag
Put the teeth up, and the regular foot on. On this setting you can do straight stitch and zigzag, giving you more control and moving the fabric in a straight line; or you can control which way the fabric moves.

The same setting on the machine is used for zigzag; but you need to change the stitch width, which will determine how wide the zigzag is.

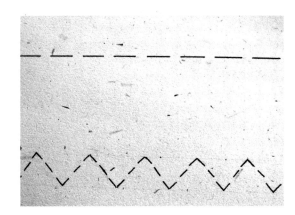

Diagram of straight stitch and zigzag stitch

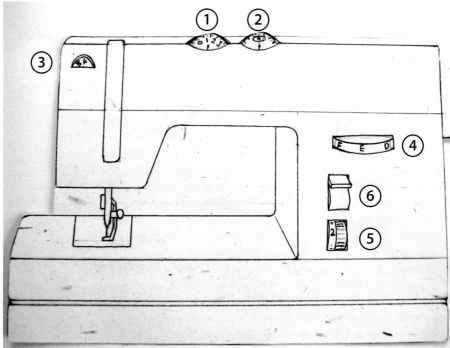

Diagram of Pfaff sewing machine

Freehand

You need the teeth down for this (normally a switch next to the teeth), the freehand foot on, and you need to work with the fabric in an embroidery hoop. Set the stitch type to straight stitch. You have less control, but a more flexible way of working.

The descriptions should be standard, but please follow individual guidelines on your sewing machine for differences. All sewing machines will have the same settings, but the position of the settings will vary from machine to machine.

1 *Stitch width dial*

When selecting the width, the needle must not be in the material. 5 is the maximum width; 0 is the minimum – this is the setting you need when using straight stitch.

2 *Needle position dial*

When the circle is in the middle (see diagram) the needle is in the central position. 14 additional needle positions can be selected by turning the needle positioning dial in gradual increments to the left or right.

3 *Setting the needle thread tension*

For normal sewing, move dial to setting 4–5. To loosen the tension, move down to 2–3 (for fabric flowers later on in the book).

4 *Utility stitches*

This setting is to change the stitch type – refer to individual sewing-machine manuals.

5 *Stitch length adjustment*

You can adjust the stitch length between 0 and 6 mm ($^1/_4$ in.) by turning the dial up or down to your required length.

6 *Reverse sewing*

The machine sews in reverse only as long as this button is pressed in. Use this button to secure stitches in place by going back and forth a couple of times.

Scissors

A range of sharp scissors is always useful, from needlework small scissors to paper scissors and crimping scissors.

Glue

Wood glue, fabric glue, Bondaweb (we will discuss this later), a glue gun (very handy for fast gluing and quick projects).

Needle and threads

A selection of hand-sewing needles and a range of threads of different thickness, such as cotton, sparkly threads and embroidery threads, will come in handy for everything, both for the sewing machine and hand embroidery.

Fabric pens, pencils and crayons

You can buy these in any haberdasher's; you can get crayons that draw onto fabric but rub off, or pens that wash off. I tend to use the rub-off ones as this method is quicker.

Vilene™ dissolvable

This is a fantastic material to work with for building up layers of stitch and fabric, and it can then be dissolved and you are left with some great effects. (See Suppliers and sources at the end of the book.)

Tapes

Sticky tape, masking tape, gaffa tape, double-sided tape. All these different tapes will come in handy for holding materials in place, sticking images on the wall for inspiration or using as a marker when painting.

DIY tools

Other tools which may come in handy depending on the task and your own projects are as follows: saw, hammer, pliers, staple gun, nails, screws, etc.

Wires

Fishing wire or line is always handy to have; you can get this from any fishing shop, which normally works out cheaper than buying it from a craft shop. Get the transparent fishing lines, which are great for hanging things without a noticeable thread. The line is normally very thin, so it can be used with a needle as if you were sewing.

Craft wire is also another good material when working with textiles as it is very versatile and can be used for many things, such as decorative flowers bound in material, or to easily join hard surfaces together.

Craft wire comes in many different thicknesses. Again, I recommend not getting this from a craft shop, but instead from a hardware shop or DIY store, as it will be cheaper.

Another, more cost-effective option is to use old wire coat hangers.

Don't worry if you haven't got all these materials; the idea of this book is to be very experimental and mix and match different techniques and ideas together to create something individual. It's up to you – your ideas, your design, your creation. Anything goes and there are no right or wrong combinations.

Each section will tell you which equipment and materials will help, but procedures and techniques are flexible. The idea is that each is cost-effective and simple, and can be adapted to your unique style and taste.

Appliqué

Appliqué comes from the French word *'appliquer'*, meaning to put or to lay on.

There are many different techniques when you appliqué, the traditional method being to stitch by hand or machine, but the type I am going to practise (using a type of iron-on adhesive applied to the backs of fabric) is a simple way of layering materials and attaching fabrics together. The adhesive, Bondaweb, allows a simple form of appliqué which is very effective and can be used to form simple or extremely decorative designs. It can also be used on a range of mixed-media materials such as leather, thin wood and thin plastic that may be too hard to stitch; Bondaweb is ideal for joining such hard materials.

YOU WILL NEED
- Bondaweb (can be bought by the metre so just buy what you think will be needed)
- fabric
- scissors
- iron
- images to work from (photos or drawings)
- protection fabric (to cover and protect your chosen design from the hot iron)

Step 1

Choose your desired fabric – refer to the Materials chapter if you need help on deciding what works well together.

Step 2

You will need some imagery to work from, for example, photos of flowers you've taken, old patterned wallpaper or even a pattern on some old fabric. It can be as simple or as detailed as you like, but bear in mind you will be cutting them out from the fabric later.

Step 3

Turn the iron to the hottest temperature.

Preparing your design

Step 4

Pick a starting fabric – sometimes it's best to be experimental and just pick randomly. Cut your fabric and Bondaweb to roughly the same size.

Step 5

The iron will now be hot enough to use. Lay the rough side of the Bondaweb down on reverse side of the fabric, and get your protective layer and lay this on top. Now you are ready to iron together. Make sure the Bondaweb and fabric are stuck well together, and remove the protective layer.

Drawing your design onto Bondaweb

Step 6

Draw your chosen design onto the paper side of the fabric, then cut it out. I often keep the designs simple and build up many layers using multiple fabrics in many patterns and colours. Your designs can get more decorative as you build up layers. A bonus when working with Bondaweb is that once glued to the fabric, the fabric does not fray when cutting out, so you achieve clean edges to your designs.

Step 7

You then need to peel off the paper from your cut-out design and lay it glue-side

Ironing the design

29

Close-up of beadwork on a Bondaweb design

down on a chosen background fabric, furniture piece or garment. You are then ready to iron down your design, making sure to use the protective layer so the iron doesn't touch your design.

Step 8

Repeat this process as many times as you wish with multiple fabrics and patterns, building up textures, colours and details in your designs.

Alternative uses

- Use Bondaweb to attach fabric to wood metal or plastic. It will stick to most materials. Iron the fabrics straight onto old lampshades or old bags, or even create your own artwork on a canvas.
- Work on top of your Bondaweb designs with different stitch techniques, hand or embroidered.
- Build up textures with beads, buttons and other bits and bobs to add detail and definition.

Plaiting & cording

YOU WILL NEED

- ▣ scissors
- ▣ strips of material
- ▣ thread
- ▣ sewing machine

Making plaits and cords is a really simple way to create designs from found fabrics. It is a versatile way to create surface texture and add interesting detail.

The first idea I will discuss is plaiting. I'm sure you all know how to plait from your school days, but I will just go through a few simple ideas of how you can use this technique.

Step 1 (for plaits)
Select three fabrics you want to work with – refer to the materials section if you are unsure. You will need long strips of fabrics to create your plaits. Try alternative materials such as old ties, strips of leather, wool or strings of old beads. Cut the strips as thick or as thin as you like, depending on how delicate you want your finished product to be.

Strips of fabric

Step 2
Plait these strips together.

Step 1 (for cords)

Select strips of a chosen fabric, the longer the better. For cording you will need to pick thinner fabrics as you will be putting them through the sewing machine.

Step 2
You will need to set up your sewing machine on a zigzag stitch, with the teeth up.

Step 3
Put one end of the fabric strip under the needle with the foot down. Start sewing

Pile of cords

whilst also twisting the fabric strip; you will need to feed the fabric through under the foot with your other hand to ensure that it runs though easily.

Step 4
When you have stitched the entire length of your fabric, twisting all the way, you can cut the thread.

With both of these techniques you can build up piles of plaited and corded strips in many colours and thicknesses. A colour idea which works well is when you use old fabrics in one colour, i.e. using many shades and different materials but all in the same colour.

Ideas with plaits and cords
* An idea which I regularly use is to wrap plaits and cords around furniture legs or arms to add texture and interesting layers. You can fit them on with fabric glue or a

glue gun, or I normally use wood glue as this dries clear and will adhere the fabric to the wood very securely.

• Use your plaits and cords as trimming around a lampshade by sewing or gluing them on.

Couching

YOU WILL NEED

▪ thick needle
▪ embroidery thread

Couching is a technique using your plaits and cords to create texture and a three-dimensional look to your textile pieces.

Step 1
Find a pattern to work from – something fairly simple to begin with. I've used stripes to build up a 3D layer.

Step 2
Choose a background fabric – a thick material will work well.

Step 3
Draw your design or pattern onto your chosen fabric with a fabric pen.

Step 4
Select your cords or plaits. If you want a more intricate pattern then use thin cords; if you want something bold and three-dimensional then use thick ones.

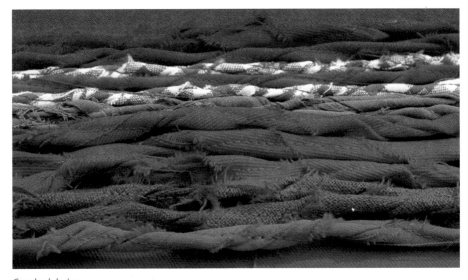

Couched design

Step 5

You then need to sew your cords on following the design, using whichever stitch you can to attach them. You may want the stitch to show as part of your design; if not try and sew underneath.

You can use this technique to build up many layers. Be selective with colours; try and stick to the colours of your design or it could end up looking like a hippy rag rug. Think about which materials you are making your cords with as this will help define the final piece.

Wrapping

Again, this technique uses strips of fabric or cords and plaits to create interesting textures and effects in a textile project. For the purpose of this section, I'm going to look at wrapping with cords, but equally you can wrap with plaits or just use strips of material.

YOU WILL NEED

- a big pile of cords (follow cords and plaits section, page 30)
- glue gun or fabric glue
- sharp scissors
- something to wrap, such as a picture frame or the arms or legs of a chair

I don't need to do a step-by-step guide for this technique as it is very simple.

You simply need to apply glue to your desired surface and wrap your cords around, overlapping them to make sure you cover all the surface underneath. A glue gun is the best method of attachment for this, though be very sure to apply it carefully as it can look messy if not neatly done.

Try sticking to a colour scheme, so when making your cords plan carefully and pick colours which either complement each other or look planned.

I use this technique to cover tatty old woodwork or colours I don't like in the old material. It builds up textures and layers and works well.

Wrapped chair leg and back

Try the same, even simpler idea of not even making cords, just picking fabric you like – make strips and wrap with this. Try wrapping with wool, string or long strips of anything else you think could work.

Found fabric flowers

This is a very simple but lovely technique to create three-dimensional flowers with found fabrics. I use them to add depth to cushions and lampshades. They can be sewn on in clusters or mixed in with beads, sequins and used with other embroidery.

YOU WILL NEED
- embroidery hoop (a range of sizes is useful)
- scissors
- fabric crayon (one that rubs off)
- different fabrics, patterned and plain
- sewing machine
- elastic thread

Step 1
Set your sewing machine to the freehand stitch, making sure you lift the teeth up, and put the correct foot in. Load the bobbin up by hand with your elastic thread; it is too springy to do on the machine. Don't pull the elastic too tight when winding it on, just add light pressure. Reduce the tension on your machine so the elastic can glide through easily.

Step 2
Stretch fabric over the embroidery hoop, making sure the fastening of the hoop is at the bottom when the two hoops are together. Pull your fabric as tight as possible; this makes it easier when you sew on top of it. You can use any fabric, but try to use something quite delicate and thin rather than a heavy fabric. I find old cotton shirts and satins and silks work well.

Step 3
Draw a very simple flower shape onto the fabric, big or small, or if you have a large hoop you can draw a few smaller. Use a fabric crayon to draw the flowers; this will rub off later. When you get confident at creating the flowers you will be able to sew them without drawing them first; it becomes easy with practice.

Stitched flowers ready to be cut out

Step 4

Place your hoop under the needle and start sewing around your flower shape; go back and forth a few times at the start to secure the stitches.

Step 5

Cut out the shape with a pair of small sharp scissors. Do this before removing the fabric from the hoop – it just makes it easier. You will then have a three-dimensional fabric flower.

Make lots of flowers in different sizes, colours and patterns, and experiment with different shapes – any simple shape will work.

You can sew them onto any background. Create an eclectic mix by building up different patterns on top of a patterned background, or create something simple using plain fabrics.

Finished 3D flowers

3D flowers sewn onto an old knitted cardigan stretched over a reclaimed lampshade

35

Make more dainty flowers by using old silks and satins, or create a bold, chunky effect using velvets, thicker cottons and old knits. This is a fantastic technique for using up all your scrap pieces of fabrics and offcuts.

Rag flowers

This is another extremely easy technique to create edging, borders or 3D effects on a design.

YOU WILL NEED
- an assortment of different fabrics
- needle
- thread

Step 1
Layer up three fabrics of your choice, and then cut out a circle about 60 cm (24 in.) in diameter. When you have created your circles, place your forefinger in the centre and cluster the fabric up around it, ruffling the fabric into your desired shape.

Step 2
Remove your finger and hold the flower underneath, as if you were holding a stumpy stem. Sew the 'stem' in place to secure the layers of fabric in the flower shape. Trim the layers of fabric to make the flower more decorative and detailed.

LEFT An assortment of rag flowers; RIGHT 3D rag flowers

More ideas for rag flowers

- Try using pinking scissors for the edges of the fabric, or cut zigzag edges along the top to create a more rustic feel.
- You can also place bits and bobs such as beads or ruffled string into the flower to create different effects.
- Try creating lots of flowers in different colours and sizes. Experiment with different shapes, materials and fabrics.
- Lace, velvet and net are great fabrics for this technique.
- I recently used this idea to create lots of flowers to decorate my sister's wedding cake. It made a bold statement and lasted much longer than fresh flowers!

Raffia or ribbon

I have boxes of bits and bobs such as old raffia, ribbons or just strips of old fabric which I like the colours of. I have collected them over time, but generally whenever I go to a scrapstore I tend to find suitable materials. I pick them up all the time and keep them for when I am making something new.

YOU WILL NEED
- sewing machine on freehand stitch
- crayon
- fabric selection of raffia, ribbons

An Irish sewing machine would be handy for this technique, but not essential.

Step 1

Design a simple pattern with a fabric crayon onto a background fabric. Choose simple bold shapes such as circles, squares or organic shapes (curved/rounded shapes rather than ridged shapes). Place your fabric in a large embroidery hoop.

Step 2

Choose a selection of raffia or ribbon to use, or a selection of both. Make sure the strips are fairly long, half a metre or so.

Step 3

The idea is to fill in the shapes drawn on the fabric by securing the raffia with freehand stitching. You need to be extremely careful with this technique, making sure your fingers are a safe distance away from the needle at all times. Secure one end of the raffia with a couple of stitches, and then begin to move your fabric in the hoop around so that you can attach the raffia all over the shape and fill it in. This could take a while, so if you prefer, pick thicker raffia or ribbon, depending on how detailed you want the final piece to be.

Flower made from raffia

You can attach the raffia in a more formal way by rotating the hoop in the same direction – this will make the final design look neater – or you can just do it freestyle and fill the gaps.

Repeat by covering your shapes with different-coloured raffia or different fabric.

In my example, I have stuck to a flower design and then added detail with hand stitches and a few small beads.

Covering found objects

I am going to demonstrate the idea of covering recycled plastic bottle tops with fabrics, to then cover an old lampshade or to decorate a picture frame or mirror. Any small objects could work well for this, such as cotton reels, buttons and large beads; however, it is probably better to find a simple shape with a smooth surface that is easy to cover.

Other ideas could be clothes pegs (the old dolly-peg-style ones could work well), lolly sticks, shapes cut from old cardboard, wrapping wire or old coat hangers with fabric.

YOU WILL NEED
- fabric – thin fabric will work better. Old tights or stretchy fabric will be good as they mould to the object well.
- bottle tops – you'd be amazed how many you can collect from milk cartons, shampoo bottles, juice containers and jam jars. The more varied they are in size the better; this will make for a more interesting final product.
- glue, fabric glue and a glue gun

Collected bottle tops

Step 1
First you need to choose which fabric you are going to use. Try to be selective about colours and pattern, and pick a colour scheme. I've chosen to work with an old pair of patterned tights and some other plain fabric.

Step 2
You need to work out the best way to cover each bottle top with fabric. I found the best way is to literally stretch the fabric over the bottle top and secure it in place with some

Bottle tops covered in fabric and old tights

fabric glue, or the glue gun if the shape or size is too difficult.

Step 3
When you have got a large selection of bottle tops covered, you can cover your surface. Think about layout and pattern – stretch out the bottle tops beforehand and use as a guide. You may want the bottle tops higgledy-piggledy, or you may decide to arrange them in a more structured format. This is where your individuality comes in! Try decorating a lampshade, or a flatter surface such as a picture frame.

More ideas for covering objects
- Try this same technique with other objects as suggested before.
- Try covering them with different materials – stick with sequins, wrap with wool, or use paint or dye if the materials are absorbent.

Reusing old rags

When in search of old and found materials, it is too easy to come across tatty, worn and shabby drab fabrics in the form of dated curtains with dodgy floral prints and no flair, old pillowcases and worn sheets. Don't be disheartened by this – instead look upon it as a challenge!

I recommend that you treat rags as blank canvases and dye them your desired colour and rework them, using them as what they originally were, or even better reinventing them and using the fabric in new and exciting ways.

The easiest way to dye natural fibres such as cotton, linen and muslin is to use Dylon dyes. Dylon has a range of different dyes suitable for various materials such as wool, wood and silk; in fact there are different dyes for almost every fabric, and they are very simple to use. Ask in the shop for the correct dye for your project, or go to their website, www.dylon.co.uk. You can buy Dylon at most larger supermarkets or craft shops, and dry cleaners also often sell it. If you can't get hold of Dylon, you should be able to get hold of a different brand. Please read all instructions before use.

Other suitable materials for dyeing include net curtains, old lace, light-coloured knitwear, etc. Any fabric that is uninspiring and needs some vibrancy added is a good candidate. There's no need to waste a thing!

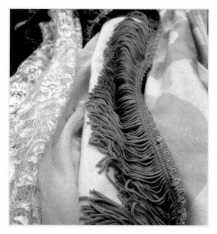

Old lifeless rags and tassels

Hand-dyeing fabrics

Revamped fabric hanging out to dry

Lamps

If you are looking for old lampshades to redo, then you will almost definitely find many in drab colours with tatty edges and generally very old-fashioned in style.

Again, don't be disheartened or uninspired by this. Pull off the tassels and trimming and try dyeing these too. They are often silk or good-quality threads, so it would be a shame to simply discard them. Be experimental; materials and fabrics will vary, so you may need to try out different dyes. Try taking what you want to dye into a fabric shop and asking what dye you need for the job; normally they can help.

Scrap fabric snake draft excluders

Snake draft excluders are obviously nothing new, but this project is to remind you what to do with any old bulky fabric you may have lying around.

They are 100% recycled, made with old curtains, and stuffed with old blankets and covers.

- Simply choose your fabric and cut two lengths at your desired width.
- Sew the two lengths together inside out, making sure to leave a hole big enough to stuff, and sew a tongue at the right end pointing inwards.
- Turn the right way round and stuff with any scrap fabric.
- Sew up the hole, and sew on some eyes.

I made a whole clan of 300 snakes for an eco garden centre – made entirely from recycled curtains!

Fabric pompoms

YOU WILL NEED

 some thick card from an old cardboard box

 scissors

 strips of fabric

Fabric pompoms may sound a bit childish, but I can assure you the end results are great, and the likes of John Galliano and Toshikazu Iwaya have all created outfits for the catwalk with them. Create small ones to make a necklace or sew giant ones together to make a rug! This is a fantastic technique for using up old strips of fabric, with great results.

I think the final result is far more successful than wool ones, and you can be very creative with the fabrics you use. I have used string mixed with wool, mixed with strips of net curtain to make something a bit different.

Step 1

As in the cords and plaits section, you need to gather together lots of different fabrics of your choice and cut or tear them into strips. Make them as long as possible as this makes the next step easier.

Step 2

Draw a circle on your card; it can be as big or as small as you like, but as an example try a circle which is 40 cm (16 in.) in diameter. Then you need to draw a smaller circle inside the one you've just drawn, in this case about 15 cm (6 in.) in diameter.

Step 3

You need two of these shapes, so either lay another piece of card underneath

Pompom template to cut out

when cutting them out or cut out two separately, making sure they are the same size. Cut out the centre circles, and you should be left with a doughnut shape.

Step 4

Pick your first strip of fabric and tie the two circles together with a simple knot.

Step 5

Begin wrapping the fabric around and around, through the middle, and in and out, trying to cover the card. When you have reached the end of the first strip, tie on your next piece of fabric with a little knot and continue wrapping. Keep wrapping until you can't get any more strips through the hole.

Rag pompoms

Step 6

Tie the end anywhere you can, either to the card or to the end of another piece of fabric. Make sure it's tied tightly.

Step 7

Cut another strip of fabric which is a bit bigger than the diameter of the circle. Get your sharp scissors and begin to cut around the outside edge. The aim is to cut through to the card and to separate the two doughnut shapes.

Step 8

When you have cut into enough of the fabric to see the card, get your other strip of fabric ready, slot it in between the two pieces of card and begin to wrap it the whole way round the card.

Step 9

When one end of the fabric strip meets the other, tie the end really tightly.

Step 10

You now need to pull the card circles away from the fabric. If you do it slowly and carefully, you will be able to save the shapes to use again for the next one. You should now be left with a textured ball!

More ideas for fabric pompoms

- Try experimenting with various fabrics and different-sized circles. The more you practise, the better you become.
- Dyed net curtains are a brilliant material to cut into strips and use, or try raffia or coloured string.

Lazertran™

Lazertran™ is a type of transfer paper, and can be used to transfer images onto almost anything, from wood and plastic to ceramics or metal. Each transfer technique is different depending on the material you are transferring onto.

I am going to discuss ideas of how to use Lazertran™ with wood, as this is chiefly what I use it for – it is a great technique for wooden furniture and can create something quirky and unique. It's different and simple, and transforms dull and drab items into colourful, patterned pieces of art.

Buying Lazertran™

Lazertran™ is not the cheapest of materials to buy, so make sure you plan what you are doing carefully. The easiest way to purchase Lazertran™ is to go to their website, www.lazertran.com.

Lazertran™ printouts

There are two different types:
- one for which you use a photocopier to transfer images
- or one which you put in your computer printer.

I would recommend getting the one for your printer, as it can be hard to find places which will allow you to use it in their photocopiers. It will also be more cost-effective using your printer, as stationers will also charge you per copy.

Suitable wooden materials to work with

Lazertran™ will work on anything wooden, providing it has a smooth surface. It will also help if the shape of your chosen material is not too complicated. For example, a wooden box or rectangular chair leg is fine, but a decorative intricate lamp stand with lots of nooks and crannies would be trickier.

If it is a shiny, painted surface, you will need to sand it down and make a rougher surface or 'key' to work on.

Getting started

First you will need to find an image to work with. Find one of the samples you have made from the previous Techniques section. One with texture and pattern will work well.

You can use any image; it doesn't have to be a mixed-media sample. I just find that using something you have created makes the final piece truly unique.

Other ideas for images include wallpaper, a pattern from a book you like or an image from an old poster – anything where there is a design that will fill up a whole page.

Scan your chosen image into the computer. It is up to you if you then manipulate it on the computer or just leave it how it is. Alternatively, you can print out a photographic image which you have taken and stored on your computer.

Put the Lazertran™ into your computer, making sure you have the paper the correct way up (see instructions on the packet), and print out your image – it's as simple as that. Or you can print out a photographic image which you have on your computer.

I'm going to show you two of my ideas when working with Lazertran™. Here I have printed out onto Lazertran™ some images I took with a camera of my wall hangings and lamp designs. These images will work well and create a 3D effect when transferred onto objects.

idea 1 Chair legs and arms

To create a truly unique chair for your home, Lazertran™ is a great way of achieving some quirky ideas. It is a highly versatile material.

YOU WILL NEED
- sandpaper
- white spirit
- paintbrush
- primer
- washing-up bowl
- water

Step 1
Find a wooden chair which has smooth legs and arms (no intricate patterns). (See previous chapters for where to source an old chair.)

Step 2
Sand the chair down with some sandpaper if it has a shiny or gloss finish. If it needs a lot of sanding, you can use an electric sander. You can buy small ones from any DIY store. I would only recommend this if you are going to be doing a lot of projects; it's not worth it for just one.

Step 3
Decide the part of the chair to which you are going to apply the Lazertran™. You may want to do the whole chair. I like to cover just a part, for instance a section of the leg or part of the arm, and then paint, upholster or use other techniques on the rest. As discussed earlier, Lazertran™ is not cheap, so be careful when deciding how much you want to use.

Step 4

I find that giving the wood a coat of white primer paint really helps as an undercoat and acts as a contrast, so that when you put on your Lazertran™, it really shows up. If you apply it directly to the wood or to a dark colour, the colours of your design can be drab and get lost.

Step 5

Wait for your primer to dry – it is best to leave it for 24 hours.

Primed chair leg

Step 6

Cut the Lazertran™ with your image on to the right size – i.e. enough to wrap around a leg, or the right shape to lie across part of the arm.

Step 7

Paint some white spirit onto the section.

Step 8

Soak the Lazertran™ in some water and wait for it to start coming away from the backing paper. It will be translucent and very thin.

Step 9

Very carefully take the Lazertran™ out of the water and apply it to the section coated with white spirit. It can rip very easily, so handle with care and make sure you have it in position before securing it in place.

Cutting out Lazertran™ to size

Step 10

Paint over gently with white spirit to set it into place.

Step 11

When it is completely dry apply some clear varnish on top; this will protect the wood from getting easily scratched.

Continue this process as many times as you like on chairs, lamp stands or any wooden furniture.

Fixing the Lazertran™ with white spirit

idea 2 Unique imagery with Lazertran™

I particularly like creating quirky imagery, which I then scan in, or photograph, and print out onto Lazertran™. I enjoy the effect of building up layers and almost unfolding a story.

Using 3D objects of textiles pieces as a starting point and then scanning them or photographing them creates unusual effects that can be applied to wood and furniture – although the end result is flat, it gives an illusion of being 3D.

Here is an idea with wood to create an interesting effect.

YOU WILL NEED
- a sheet of very thin wood – e.g. veneer sheets (see suppliers at the end of the book), or some old lolly sticks which you can break or cut up
- paint – any kind, although acrylic or household emulsion will work well
- paintbrush
- scissors
- something to create texture such as a knife or some kind of pointy instrument

Step 1

Create a texture with a chosen colour of paint by applying the paint thickly to the wooden surface and using a knife or the end of something pointy to introduce streaks, spots, lines or scratches into the paint. Leave to dry.

Painted textured wooden squares

Step 2

Cut out shapes from the wood using your scissors, or try snapping the wood. Layer your cut-out shapes in the desired pattern on a sheet of paper or card (or directly onto your scanner).

Step 3

Either take a picture of your design and load it onto your computer, or lay it in the scanner and then print the images out onto Lazertran™.

Step 4

Use Lazertran™ in the same way as in Idea 1, above, and then use the imagery on a chair leg or arm.

Wooden square imagery transferred onto a chair with Lazertran™

In the following chapters there are more unique ways of working with Lazertran™.

Pleating

Pleating is a simple yet beautiful idea, which can be used to create delicate effects or bold statements depending on the fabric you choose to use.

YOU WILL NEED
- strips of fabric – thinner fabric will work better
- sewing machine on straight stitch
- background fabric – it doesn't matter about the colour or design, as it is just a background for the pleats to be sewn onto

Step 1
Create a big pile of strips of fabric, as you did for the plaits and cords section. Make the strips about 5 cm (2 in.) wide; it doesn't matter too much, but don't make them too thin. I have chosen one kind of fabric for a change and made lots of strips from it. Pick a fabric that is easy to tear as this will make the job much quicker. My fabric was old polyester shirts – perfect for the job!

Step 2
Lay a strip onto the background fabric, running up one edge. Put one end under the foot of the sewing machine and secure it with a stitch.

Step 3
You then need to make a fold in the strip, pleating it back on itself to create the first pleat, making sure you still keep the background fabric flat to the sewing machine.

Step 4
Continue to do this until the strip of fabric has run out. If it runs out before you reach the end of the background fabric, simply join another strip onto it.

Step 5
Start another strip next to your first strip, and repeat the process to create lines of pleats. Try to slightly overlap the strips so the background fabric is not seen. It sounds complicated but when you see the image overleaf it will make sense.

When you have finished you should have created a mass of layered, pleated strips which should give a beautiful ruffled effect.

You can now continue layering or adding contrasting fabrics, or leave it as one colour or pattern. You can also try sewing on the strips in diagonals or in curves.

Pleating with old white, beige and leopard-pattern shirts

Slashing & layering

Slashing and layering mixes ideas of embroidery, appliqué and collaging multiple layers of fabric. It's a good technique for mixing and matching fabric and working with clashing patterns.

I am going to go through three different ideas for slashing and layering; they are all very simple, but the end results can achieve very different looks for a variety of interior products such as lampshades, cushions or seat covers.

idea 1 Slashed stripes

YOU WILL NEED

- scissors
- two pieces of rectangular fabric
- straight stitch on the sewing machine

Step 1
Choose two different patterned fabrics and place them on top of one another. I think clashing and contrasting ones work best together, or you may like to mix spots and stripes, or mix a black and white layer with a coloured layer.

Slashed and layered fabric

Step 2

Select a small straight stitch on your sewing machine.

Step 3

Put one corner end of the layered material under the foot of the sewing machine and do a running stitch in a straight line, running from one end to the other. When you have reached one end, then turn the fabric so that you can now do a 1 cm ($^3/_8$ in.) margin stitch along the top end, turn your fabric once again and do another running stitch all the way back to the other end running parallel with the other line. Repeat all the way across the fabric. When you are finished, you should have stripes in thread. It is up to you how apart you do the running stitches, but I suggest about a 1–2 cm ($^3/_8$–$^3/_4$ in.) space.

Step 4

The idea for this step is to cut away the top layer of fabric and to reveal the underlying pattern or colour. Using some small sharp scissors, cut slits in between the sewn lines, being very careful not to cut a hole in the bottom fabric, or to cut the thread. Try to trim off a bit of fabric in between each sewn line to expose the fabric underneath.

You can make the sewn lines as close or as far apart as you like, depending on the desired finished effect. You can also layer up more than two fabrics and cut through to expose more colours and patterns.

idea 2 **Pintuck with slashing**

YOU WILL NEED
- same as Idea 1

Follow Steps 1 and 2 from previous Idea 1, but choose larger fabric this time, about 50 x 50 cm (20 x 20 in.).

Step 3

Fold your fabric over and away from you about 3–4 cm (1 $^1/_4$ x 1 $^5/_8$ in.) from the edge, and sew a running stitch really close to the outside folded edge. When you have finished the stitching, cut the thread and secure ready for the next line.

Step 4

Keep folding your fabric over about 3–4 cm (1$^1/_4$ x 1$^5/_8$ in.), doing the same running stitch on the outside folded edge, about half a centimetre (less than $^1/_4$ in.) in.

Slashed pintucks

Step 5

When you have gone all the way along, open your fabric out and you should have created a 3D effect with ridges sticking outwards from the fabric. The fabric at this stage is called a 'pintuck'.

Step 6

Now get your scissors and very carefully cut a tiny slither of fabric away by sewing each line, to expose the underneath fabric.

You should have created a technique similar to Idea 1, but this time with a 3D effect.

idea 3 Diagonal pintuck slashing

YOU WILL NEED
- same as Idea 1

Follow Steps 1–5 of Idea 2 to create pintuck fabric, but make the 3D fabric ridges higher by doing the running stitch further in – about 1 cm ($^3/_8$ in.) rather than half a centimetre.

Step 6

Put your fabric back under the sewing machine with the sewn lines parallel from left to right. Secure a few stitches in the bottom right-hand corner.

Step 7

You now need to do a running stitch up the fabric, folding the slits of the fabric away from you to expose the layer underneath. The bottom part of the slit will have stayed flat, and the top part will have been pushed back and sewn down.

Step 8

When you reach the end of that running stitch, turn your fabric to a right angle and do another running stitch along the top of the fabric for about 3–4 cm ($1^1/_4$–$1^5/_8$ in.).

Step 9

Turn your fabric through 90 degrees again, but this time, when you are doing the running stitch, pull the bottom flap of the slit towards you to expose the under fabric, and sew the top part of the slit down, exposing the top fabric.

LEFT Pintuck zigzag; RIGHT Zigzag pintuck on patchwork fabric

Zigzag slashed fabric

Repeat Steps 7, 8 and 9 all the way along the fabric until you reach the end. You should be left with a diagonal sewn slashed piece of fabric, which can give a textured, unusual effect.

Try the same technique of sewing the ridges diagonally without slashing the fabric first. For this you only need one layer of fabric, so you can also make the ridges more detailed as it will be easier to sew into thinner fabric.

In these examples I have first created a patchwork striped effect with a range of fabrics. I achieved this by sewing different materials together and using the diagonal pintuck on top.

Patchwork fabric with pintuck for a chair seat

idea 4 Patchwork with pintuck

Create a patchwork of fabric by choosing a range of different colours or patterns which work well together. Join them in an unusual or unexpected way, such as on the diagonal, with stripes of different thickness, or randomly.

Follow Steps 1–5 in Idea 2 to create pintucks. This idea works well for covering a chair seat.

idea 5 Freehand shapes and slashing

Try layering up different fabrics, putting them in an embroidery hoop, drawing a design on the sewing machine with the freehand stitch, and then cutting out different layers of the fabric to expose the different materials. Circles work well for this technique; for each circle cut out different layers of the fabric to give an eclectic finish.

6 ideas with...

This chapter explores using techniques from the previous chapters, but looking more specifically at certain fabrics and materials.

For each material I will explore possible techniques and potential products for which the method could be used.

Topics explored will be:

- pegs
- old knits
- found ties
- cutlery
- reused leather
- second-hand shirts

Pegs

Pegs and lolly sticks

Whether you have old dolly pegs, new wooden pegs, lolly sticks or any small wooden bits and bobs that need something creative doing with them, then the following ideas are some good ways of making something quirky and unusual.

They can then be used to make a picture, or I have used them as the trimming of a lampshade.

idea 1 Lazertran™

As in the previous Techniques chapter, use Lazertran™ to cover wooden pegs. It's quite fiddly, but it achieves good results, and it's a good way of adding 3D, picture or textiles effects to a flat surface.

Follow the steps in the Techniques section for using Lazertran™, or follow the instructions provided in the Lazertran™ packet.

idea 2 Paint

Use any paint you can find – acrylic or poster paints work well, or I often use tester household emulsion paints as you can get them in almost any colour.

You can get household emulsion and gloss in all sizes of tins.

Dyed and painted lolly sticks

If you use a lot of paint in your work, there are places you can now get all sorts of old paint, donated by painters and decorators, for free. Find out where your nearest scrapstore is, or ask at your local tip. I've previously decorated whole houses with free second-hand paint, which not only saves you money but also helps to reduce waste in the environment.

To decorate the pegs with paint, you simply need to get a small brush and paint them. If you are painting lots, you may want to dip them in the paint and allow drips to drop. The best way to do this is to tie a piece of string or thread around them and dip them in the paint pot. Hang them out on a line to dry with newspaper placed below, or place them to dry on a sheet of plastic.

idea 3 Dye

You can buy Dylon™ dyes and dissolve in water, or I use powdered dye (Disperse™). You may have used these at a university or workshop.

Add a tiny amount to a medium-sized bowl of lukewarm water, so that the dye dissolves. Add the wooden pegs, leave for a few minutes, then take out.

Leave to dry on some newspaper. Once they are dry, the dye will have stained them and it shouldn't come off.

Try dyeing different things, such as lolly sticks and small pieces of wood. I had some wooden buttons which dyed successfully. Experiment with different colours.

Varnish your pegs if you want a glossy effect, and also to protect them.

Dyed and painted dolly pegs

idea 4 Wrap or cover

Collect some thin and fine fabric in your chosen colours, or gather some threads and wool.

This idea is very simple. Glue one end of the wooden object and wrap your wool, thread or fabric round, overlapping it until you have covered the object then glue the end in place.

Mix the different materials together and come up with a colour scheme for a more distinctive final result.

Mixing the different techniques together can look effective – some painted, some dyed and some wrapped.

Use the wrapping or covering ideas in any way you like, or use my lampshade for inspiration. On this page are examples of a range of lampshades I created with dyed, painted and wrapped dolly pegs and lolly sticks I am currently producing a huge chandelier using the same effect.

LEFT Pegs on knitted lampshade; CENTRE Lampshade made of lolly sticks; RIGHT Lamp stand and shade using dyed pegs as a trim

Old knits

Whether you've got some old knitted socks that need throwing out, or you stumble across an oversized granny cardigan at a jumble sale, old knits are a fantastic and versatile fabric to manipulate. I'm going to explore two ideas with an old chunky-knit cardigan.

idea 1 Using an old knit as a background for appliqué

YOU WILL NEED
- knitted cardigan or jumper
- other fabrics – patterned or coloured which complement the wool
- Bondaweb
- iron
- scissors

Step 1
First you need to decide on a design or a pattern to work from. Refer to the Becoming inspired chapter if you are having difficulties. I have worked from a photograph of flowers and stylised it.

Step 2
Select some other fabric, for example old shirts, curtains or any scraps you have left over from other projects.

Step 3
Once you have determined what your final product is going to be, cut your knitted material to your desired size.

Step 4
You now need to refer to the Techniques chapter, and follow the instructions for using Bondaweb using the knitted cardigan as your background.

Try layering up different knitted materials in different colours and different-sized wool. Layer up a chunky knit with a fine knit. If you decide to layer up wool, make sure the Bondaweb is securely ironed down, as knitted wool can easily fray, and the Bondaweb prevents this from happening.

To make sure your design is absolutely secure, put your fabric in a hoop and stitch around the edges with your sewing machine.

Using knitting as a background for appliqué

idea 2 Rag holes in old knits

A good technique for creating controlled, fabric-trimmed holes in an old chunky knit jumper or cardigan.

YOU WILL NEED

- chunky knit
- thin strips of fabric
- big needle
- scissors

Step 1

Prepare some very thin strips of fabric, which you can either tear or cut. Make them roughly 1–2 cm (³/₈–³/₄ in.) wide.

61

Rag-stitched holes in old knitted jumper

Step 2

With care, cut a little hole in your knitted fabric. You will only need to snip it as it will begin to unravel.

Step 3

Thread the needle with a strip of fabric and tie a big knot in one end.

Step 4

Begin to sew round the hole with big stitches which go through the hole, then under and over the edge. Keep repeating, gradually pulling out the knitted fabric to make a circle.

Step 5

Sew in and out around the hole until you have secured it and stopped the knitting from fraying. You will probably need to use multiple strips to finish – so when one runs out, tie on another one and continue.

Step 6

Repeat with as many holes as you like.

Either keep the holes open and stretch over a lampshade to give light effects, or layer up with a different fabric underneath.

Rag-stitched holes layered with fabric

Found ties

Whenever you go to a charity shop or jumble sale, you are bound to find a dodgy collection of clashing and mix 'n' match men's ties – diamonds, checks, stripes and spots – but these are just the job for the following ideas.

Strike a deal when buying them – I got a whole sack for just a few pounds.

A pile of old ties

idea 1 Pleated ties

YOU WILL NEED

- a mix of ties
- straight stitch on your sewing machine

Step 1

Choose a selection of different ties. It doesn't matter if they are horrid patterns, as somehow the design will still work.

Step 2

Secure one end of the tie with a few stitches on the sewing machine.

Step 3

Sew in a straight line for about 3 cm (1¼ in.) and then fold the tie back on itself (refer to the Pleating section in the Techniques chapter for a reminder of the method). You can either pleat the ties onto a background or pleat each one individually and attach them to a chosen background afterwards. They look great together when using clashing patterns. Or try to be more selective and collect ones that match – for example, all spots or all stripes – or select similar colours.

Pleating a tie

A pile of pleated ties

idea 2 Flowers made from ties

YOU WILL NEED

- ties
- needle
- thread

This is very simple. Sculpt a flower shape by rolling up a tie into a coil, and secure the bottom with a few hand stitches. Add detail inside, such as a few beads or some stitch detail. Alternatively, create pleated ties, and then follow the above to create pleated flowers – this is more detailed than the first idea. Again hand-stitch to secure.

idea 3 Woven ties

YOU WILL NEED

- five or more ties
- straight stitch on the sewing machine, or a needle and thread

Step 1
Make a layer of ties in lines next to each other.

Step 2
Take one of your other ties and weave it in and out of the bottom layer to create a weave. Repeat this with all the ties across.

Step 3
Secure together with tacking stitches, and then sew together on the machine.

This would make a great cushion cover. If you don't have enough ties, use a different material for the back of the cushion, or use the woven ties as a background to appliqué onto, or layer up with other designs.

Ties woven together

FACING PAGE Flowers made from ties

Cutlery

This may sound like a strange material to work with, but it is something you will find in every charity shop, jumble or car-boot sale. For some reason people are always throwing out cutlery!

I recently made a chandelier from old spoons, forks and knives; it looks quirky, and also creates great light effects when you hang a lit bulb through it.

idea 1 Collecting decorative spoons

Decorative spoons can be collected very cheaply. Normally, the best bargains are found when you root around boxes at car-boot sales. They will probably be mixed with all sorts of other bits and bobs, but this is the best way to get a bargain. Negotiate a price, get a job lot.

Also, rummage around boxes of normal cutlery, as the spoons are often mixed up in there.

Be careful when sourcing spoons from charity shops as sometimes they will display them in a cabinet at the front and charge triple the price. Obviously some spoons are silver and collector's items, and therefore will be a lot more expensive. The best tip is to rummage, offer less if you buy in bulk and, finally, always haggle.

I like buying spoons that are a bit rusty or worn as I think this adds to the final effect. But if you prefer them clean, you can polish them.

Junk-shop teaspoons

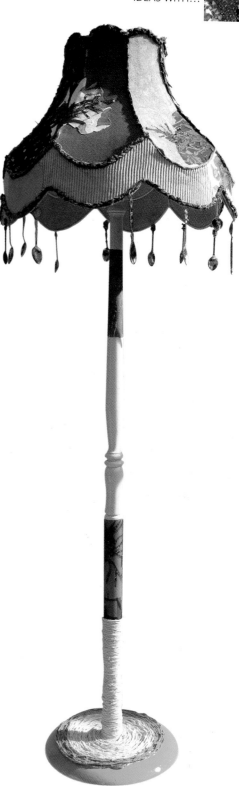

YOU WILL NEED

- decorative spoons
- tiny (smallest you can get) drill with a fine metal drill bit
- sticky tape (masking or Sellotape)
- block of wood
- small clamp
- strong thread or fishing wire
- old lampshade

Step 1

Wrap a small amount of tape around the end of the spoon handle, or wherever you plan to drill a hole.

Step 2

Clamp the spoon into place on top of the piece of wood and hold it in place against a secure surface such as a table.

Step 3

Drill a small hole in the end of the spoon on top of where you've taped, using the tape to grip the drill bit. Be extremely careful when drilling as it can slip, so take it slowly. Sometimes it can be difficult to drill the spoon if there is a decorative motif on the end. You can either drill through the motif (it may become loose) or choose a different place to put the hole. It doesn't matter if the holes are all in different places as this adds to the quirkiness.

Step 4

Thread with strong thread or fishing wire, and hang from an old lampshade to create an unusual frill. You will need quite a lot of spoons to go all the way round, and it does look better the more spoons you have.

Reclaimed lamp stand and shade with spoons as tassels

idea 2 Covering and wrapping cutlery with found fabric

For this technique, pick plain cutlery with no decoration as you will be covering it.

YOU WILL NEED
- Selection of different fabrics (choose thin fabrics)
- old cutlery (spoons, forks, knives)
- fabric glue
- small sharp scissors

Step 1
Cut your fabric roughly to fit over the chosen piece of cutlery.

Step 2
Cover your piece of fabric with a thin layer of fabric glue; you will find it easier to apply the glue with a small brush.

Step 3
Stick the fabric over the cutlery and leave to dry.

Step 4
When dry, use your small sharp scissors to cut away any excess fabric.

Cover each piece of cutlery in different material to create an eclectic effect, or use similar colours and designs to make a more controlled finished piece.

Use in the same way as in Idea 1 above, and hang from a lampshade, or make a quirky chandelier. Alternatively, you could simply use them as decoration, or frame them with a coloured background.

You could also work with papier mâché, and create a similar effect with old newspaper or magazines, then paint, dye or decorate on top.

RIGHT *Fabric-covered cutlery*

FACING PAGE *Cutlery chandelier*

Leather

This section looks at how to use old leather in a simple way. You can pick up old leather scraps from scrapstores and you can often get offcuts from fabric shops. However, you can still be charged quite a bit for this, as good-quality leather doesn't come cheap.

So for best value and varied choice I suggest you look for old leather clothes which you can cut up and use. Fake leather and suede also looks good, and you can find this in many colours. The best places to get old clothes are jumble sales, where you can buy in bulk and get a whole bag full very cheaply. You can get dubious leather jackets from the 1980s, fake-leather handbags in an array of synthetic colours or old belts. They are all great things to collect to then cut up and reinvent.

Alternatively, as mentioned earlier, go to a scrapstore and see if they have a swap shop where you can go and help yourself for free.

idea 1 Shapes and layering

YOU WILL NEED

- an assortment of different leathers
- scissors
- fabric crayon
- Bondaweb or needle and thread

Leather or fake leather will not fray, which makes it an ideal material for working with when wanting to create tough, strong, 3D shapes or images.

Step 1

Choose a design to work from; I've picked a repeat pattern which can be layered up.

Step 2

Draw your design onto the leather, being sure that when you repeat the pattern or shape you use as much fabric as you can – try to draw in all the gaps so as not to waste fabric. Draw onto different colours and textures of leather to make your design more varied.

Step 3

Get some sharp scissors and cut out your shapes.

Layers of leather shapes

Step 4

Arrange and layer up your design onto a background fabric, overlapping each cut-out image to create a 3D effect

Step 5

You now need to attach the leather to the background. To do this you only need to attach the top of each image so the bottoms are left unattached and flapping loose. It is up to you whether you decide to glue the shapes down or hand-stitch them; you could even machine them down depending on how thick your chosen leather is.

I have used this technique to layer up shapes for a wall-hanging using a background material of canvas, which holds the leather well and keeps it upright.

idea 2 Creating a whole design from leather

This is very much like appliqué, but could potentially look very high-end if you pick the right materials.

YOU WILL NEED
- selection of different leather or fake leather
- Bondaweb
- scissors
- fabric crayon

Step 1

Pick a design; you could use something from one of the previous chapters or create something new. I always think organic shapes work well when cutting shapes out in fabric. The curves and circles appear more natural, as opposed to hard geometrical shapes, but use whatever pleases you.

Step 2

Draw your design onto the back of the leather, and cut the shapes out.

Step 3

Layer them up onto a background. The more layers you do, the more intricate your design will look. Now either stitch them or glue them down with Bondaweb or a glue gun, depending on the thickness of your leather.

Mix and match the leather with more delicate fabrics and materials for a more intricate effect.

Again, I used this technique on a stiff wall-hanging, which held the leather well.

idea 3 Creating cut-through shapes in leather

A very simple idea with leather is to cut shapes and patterns with a sharp craft knife to expose patterns underneath.

In this example I re-covered a chair seat in some old worn blue suede, cutting out floral patterns to expose the old original chair fabric underneath. This redesigns the chair but also means it retains a sense of its history.

Cord-wrapped chair arm; RIGHT *Cut-out suede shapes (detail)*

Shirts

You will never go short of finding old shirts. The best way to get hold of some is to ask around your friends and family, as people often have surplus ones which they are happy to give away. This is the cheapest option. However, if you can't do this, the next best way of getting hold of some would be from a jumble sale. Try to pick out the really big sizes as you'll get more for your money! Charity shops can now charge quite a lot.

Shirts come in every check, pattern, stripe and gingham you can think of, and they look great when you mix the different patterns together. The other great thing about using shirts is that there need be no waste – use the sleeves, cuffs and buttons and design something unique. Pick the buttons from lots of different shirts and get a collection going for other projects.

Use the shirt material for techniques in the previous chapters such as appliqué, pleats, cords; in fact, you can use it for anything.

Here I have re-covered a whole chair by using old shirts (black-checked for the appliqué flowers), and I've even kept the pockets on, which I think adds to the design and the appeal. I've reused the buttons and moved them to different places, and used the hems of the shirts to wrap around the chair legs and the lamp stand.

When using appliqué with shirt fabrics, you can just keep building up multiple layers of different patterns to create detail and depth.

Another design I have devised uses different-patterned shirt fabrics to make 3D flowers on cushions.

Shirts used to decorate an old chair

Shirt cushions

Shirts used to decorate a lampshade

This is another example of a lampshade which has been revamped using old shirts.

7 revamping interior products

There are hundreds of books out there telling you how to make a cushion or how to upholster a chair – this chapter is not going to be about that, but instead will hopefully inspire you. If you decide to have a go at making a cushion or upholstering a chair, you'll be able to do it with the more imaginative fabrics and designs you have created.

Absolutely everything I use in this chapter is found, recycled, reclaimed or free!

Blinds

Whenever I look in a skip or go to the tip (which is probably, unhealthily, too often!) I seem to come across discarded blinds of all varieties – bamboo, canvas, metal or slatted. More often than not they are in a perfectly good condition, and this is an awful waste.

Why not revamp and regenerate them into a piece of art or rework them for your window. You can normally cut simple blinds such as the bamboo ones down to the correct size.

idea 1 Paint

It might sound too obvious, but if you end up stumbling across an old bamboo blind, then painting it is a simple solution for revamping it.

For my blind I used household emulsion painted on in blocks to create a simple design. You could either leave it like this or layer it with some of the other following ideas.

Bamboo blind

idea 2 Textile texture

Go through some of the previous techniques in the Techniques and Ideas with…. chapters and see what might suit your designs – 3D flowers, wrapping sections, Lazertran™ on parts of it, etc.

In this example I have stitched pleated strips onto the blind in organic shapes.

Pick colours for the strips that complement the background blind. Pleat the strips, following the step-by-step guide in the pleating section of the Techniques chapter, but don't sew them onto a background. Build up a pile of different-width pleated strips, different colours and different lengths. Either sew them onto the bamboo blind or glue them, depending on how strong you want it to be.

Ruffles and pleats used to revamp an old blind

idea 3 Re-cover

If you find an old canvas blind it is very simple to re-cover it in a chosen material and then elaborate on this by adding some other techniques ideas.

In my example, I have used Bondaweb to attach a layer of old materials such as knitted jumpers, old skirts, shirts and ties, and built up from this with pleated ties, layered leather and appliqué, then added detail with beads and stitching on top.

Canvas blinds are ideal to work on as they are perfect for a strong, sturdy background and can hold multiple layers of fabric. They form a nice wall-hanging or can be used in a window. A restaurant bought a collection of mine to hang in their windows as they still let in subtle light.

A close-up detail of a wall-hanging

FACING PAGE A revamped, reclaimed blind

You could also make a frame from reclaimed wood, attach your blind onto a backing board and then hang it on a wall. Paint your frame, or decorate it to incorporate it into the textile design – this will make a unique piece of art for a wall.

Chairs

Chairs are another thing you will not have to look too far to find. People throw them in skips, leave them for the binmen, occasionally just abandon them outside their houses – mind you, I would check with the owner before assuming you can help yourself! And again, there will be a surplus supply of them at the tip waiting to be crushed – stop, rescue them, and follow the next set of ideas.

I'm not going to explain how to upholster a chair, as that is another whole book in itself. I am just going to suggest a few innovative ways to revamp one.

idea 1 Lazertran™

If you have an old wooden chair, which is normally the type you find, you can use Lazertran™ on the legs and arms to create an illusion of textiles and texture.

I try to stick to something quite uncomplicated so it still looks high quality and doesn't clash with the actual textiles. It is just a nice effect, and often people are unsure how it's been created. For example, if I design a chair and I want the seat to be knitted, I will look at how I can make the legs look knitted without actually knitting them!

Lazertran™ is a great way to achieve such an effect. You could scan in some knitting or a knitted jumper and print it out onto Lazertran™, and then place it on your chair. This will then give the desired effect.

Refer back to the Techniques chapter for how to use Lazertran™, and always read the instructions provided on the packet.

idea 2 Covering the seat

In this example I have used the slashing and layering technique on some blue suede, which shows through the navy and white pattern underneath, the remnants of an old shirt. I created the fabric with the size of the chair seat in mind and then upholstered the fabric onto the chair.

You can either get a book to learn this, or I did a ten-week evening course to learn the basics. You can also do intensive residential courses to learn – look online for furniture restoration courses to find your local venue.

You can also re-cover with a piece of material and cut out shapes to expose the original pattern and fabric underneath. Leather is a good fabric for this as it is easy to cut with a Stanley knife and it won't fray.

Revamped chair using multiple techniques

If you find a chair that has a pop-out seat, this is great as it makes life easier if you simple want to re-cover it. This is where a staple gun will come in handy!

idea 3 Old jumpers

Try stretching an old jumper over the seat and sewing the sides down, or stapling it to the underside of the chair seat.

Jumper stretched over an old chair seat

idea 4 Old shirts

Again, if your chair has a pop-out seat, try slotting it into an old shirt with the buttons along the top, and sew the sides to the right side. Add some appliqué or some stitch detail.

idea 5 Wrapping

As already suggested earlier on, you can use a staple gun or glue gun and wrap your plaits or strips of material around the chair legs or arms, making sure you carefully cover the staples or glue . This is a good way of covering up damaged, dirty or stained chairs, and an easy way to add textiles to modern metal chair legs.

Use rolls of wool or thick thread to achieve a similar effect, create stripes, and experiment with different colour tones. This makes a nice change to simply painting the chair legs, and gets rid of the typical utilitarian brown which 'junk' chairs so often are.

Wrapped chair arm

Cushions

Very often I don't make my own cushion covers – instead I revamp old ones. I seem to stumble across lots of old cushion covers in quite nice colours and inoffensive designs, which can be easily updated or re-covered. Or it can be easy to re-dye the material to give it a new lease of life.

idea 1 Appliqué old cushion covers

To do this you need to remove the stuffing from the old cover. You may want to unstitch the sides of the cushion so you have a flat piece of fabric, or you can keep it sewn up as a cushion.

Refer to the Appliqué section in the Techniques chapter for the appliqué method. It is a good idea to try and stitch down some of the fabric, as obviously these cushions need to be fairly hard-wearing and not fall apart. Either hand-stitch them or run some of the edges under the sewing machine.

Appliquéd cushions

idea 2 Knitted cushions

As with the seat covers, why not try the same idea with old cushions? Simply take an old jumper or cardigan, measure an existing cushion which you want to re-cover, and make a new cushion cover with the old knit.

Decorate with other ideas from the Techniques chapter. I particularly like bold designs and adding 3D techniques such as pompoms on the corners, or areas covered in tactile flowers.

Lampshades

Old lampshades

Throughout the book I have discussed many techniques and ideas, for most of which, when making, I had a lampshade in mind as the final product. In my own practice I spend a lot of time rejuvenating old lampshades and lighting features, partly because they are a versatile product to work with but mainly because there is an abundance of old lampshades out there. In all the places I've listed to source materials, you can be sure to find lampshades. They come in all shapes and sizes, colours and patterns. It seems such a shame to let them go to waste when it can be so simple to reinvent them.

idea 1 Stretch knit over them

In previous chapters, I discussed reusing old knitted materials such as jumpers and dated cardigans. Now here's your chance to use those concepts to transform an old lampshade. Knitted fabric is brilliant to use for lampshades, as the light shines through the holes and you can achieve very appealing effects.

YOU WILL NEED
- lampshade
- old knitted jumper
- thick embroidery thread
- big needle

Step 1
Find a tatty old lampshade, the scruffier the better, as all you're going to be using is the frame. Old knits make a perfect new cover as the material is stretchy and can be made to go a long way, depending on how big you want the holes in the knit to be.

Step 2
Cut all the old fabric away from the lampshade. As mentioned above, all you want to be left with is the metal frame. If you want to be extra 'eco', reuse the old lampshade fabric for some of the other techniques.

Step 3
Get your jumper and find the best part to stretch over the shade. If it is particularly stretchy, you may even be able to use one of the arms – this is sometimes big enough if you have a medium-sized shade.

Make sure you pull the fabric all the way over, and leave plenty of extra so you can easily sew it onto the frame.

Step 4

Get a long piece of thick embroidery thread which matches the knit, and begin to sew around, attaching the jumper to the lampshade frame, making sure to tuck in any tatty edges and sew any loose bits of knitted material to the frame. Cut off excess bits of the jumper as you go. Make sure you sew all the way up each rung of the frame. This will take some time, but it's essential to retain the shade of the lampshade.

Jumper sleeve lampshade with 3D flowers

This technique looks particularly good on unusual-shaped shades, which tend to be the more old-fashioned ones. In my example, I have used an old, black zip-up cardigan and stretched it over a lampshade and then made a trim with rag-fabric flowers made of lace and soft fabrics.

Step 5

Now you have covered your lampshade, use some of the techniques you have learned to decorate the shade. For instance, use fabric flowers, pleated ties around the edge, tie flowers arranged around the bottom and top or any other ideas you liked the sound of and want to experiment with; be bold or stick to a more subtle approach.

Old cardigan lampshade

idea 2 Pleated ties stitched on

YOU WILL NEED

- pleated ties in various colours and patterns
- a selection of other pleated strips
- lampshade
- pins
- big needle
- embroidery thread
- scissors

Step 1

Choose a selection of pleated ties (see the Ties section of the Ideas with... chapter), and some strips of other pleated fabric to use as a background colour.

Step 2

Pick your lampshade; it might be easier to start off with a smallish one, as this is quite tricky. Pin the ties and the other pleated fabric on alternately around the shade. I used the normal pleated fabric as a background colour, and placed the ties on the top layer to form a bit of a pattern. It can be quite tough pinning the ties, so be patient and pin them on as firmly as possible so they don't come off.

Pleated ties pinned onto a lampshade

Step 3

Thread your needle with thread that roughly matches the ties. Begin to sew them onto the frame. This again is a bit tough as the ties are thick, but persevere as the end result will look really good! Make sure you sew in, or cut off, any loose ends.

When you have completed your tie lampshade, why not try making a stand to match?

FACING PAGE Tie lampshade

idea 3 Appliquéing an existing lampshade

This is a fantastic idea for covering another drab lampshade. It is fairly simple if you have the right materials.

YOU WILL NEED
- lampshade
- iron (travel iron if you have one, but not essential)
- Bondaweb
- selection of fabric
- strips of fabric
- scissors
- needle
- thread

Step 1
Cover some chosen fabric in Bondaweb. The idea is to re-cover each section of the lamp in a different colour or pattern, Bondawebbing the new material on top of the old lampshade fabric.

Step 2
Iron on the fabric in sections. This can be a bit tricky, as the iron is quite bulky and can't get in all the gaps – a small travel iron comes in very handy for this technique.

Step 3
Follow the steps in the Appliqué section of the Techniques chapter to come up with a design, whether it is geometric, flowers or organic shapes. Choose fabrics which contrast with your chosen background.

Step 4
Bondaweb on these cut-out pieces of fabric. Overlap different materials to give an eclectic feel or arrange the fabrics to complement each other.

Step 5
Trim any hanging edges with small sharp scissors.

Step 6
Revisit the Plaiting and cording section of the Techniques chapter and create some plaits or cords to use as edging. This will really finish off the shade and make it look neater and more professional. Attach your plaits or cords with stitches, or, if they are thick, you can use a glue gun as you won't be able to see the glue when they are stuck down.

Step 7
Add detail with a few little beads or stitching. Do this by using a small needle and thread, making sure to attach them securely.

Table lamp revamped with appliqué

More ideas for transforming lamps

Why not try any of the ideas from the book to transform an old lamp stand to go with your lampshade – Lazertran™, wrapping with plaits, or covering with bits and bobs you've collected and painted or dyed.

Lazertran™ on a reclaimed lamp stand

8 experimenting with furniture – the hybrid

Throughout this book virtually all discussion has revolved around novel ways of using materials. The intention has been to experiment with and revive the abandoned and derelict goods we find all around us, and to look at materials in innovative ways.

I have attempted to stimulate discussion and thinking on relatively simple levels and to inspire your own imagination. It can be difficult with our busy lives to stop and reflect for a while without thinking about the next thing we're going to do. Whatever your starting point, I hope you have felt motivated and encouraged to look at your surroundings and environment in a more open-minded way. If you have been inspired by the words, especially the photographs, you will be a convert.

In this final part I want you to consider going one step further and perhaps extending your repertoire to include slightly longer-scale projects.

Creating a 'hybrid'

A concept I have experimented with and am still exploring is making functional furniture that combines several styles to produce a new product – a 'hybrid'.

Hybrid furniture is a particular interest of mine, and it's always possible to find a wide range of suitable materials. The idea came to me when I found several broken chairs with split seats, which seemed to lend themselves to this idea.

In order to make a project like this work, you need to develop further basic skills in woodwork and metalwork. You would need to know how to use a saw, hammer and chisel, for instance, and also learn joining techniques such as forming joints, using dowels, clamping and pinning.

If you haven't yet developed the skills and you feel restricted because of this, you can always approach a local craftsperson or technician to complete this side of the project.

You are the designer, the ideas person who can then use the newly formed canvas to work on.

It is not appropriate or possible to cover this whole area in a short book, as the focus is on invention and ideas rather than woodwork and metalwork techniques. However, I do include a brief example of one of my favourite chairs. I made this by combining two pieces of furniture: a standard lamp and a simple panelled chair with a missing leg. This led to me producing an ornate reading chair which embraced many of the techniques previously covered in this book.

The hybrid chair was a fascinating and thought-provoking project because the standard lamp had to be an integral part of the chair and take the weight of a person. This meant that its construction had to be strong and durable. It is important when joining to thoroughly prepare woodwork before final assembly. Once you have a solid basic piece to work from you can then let your imagination go.

The chair and lamp were joined together using a combination of joints, glue and dowels, and bound together using the wrapping technique covered in previous chapters.

Hybrid lamp chair

Double/two-seater chair

Take it further

My double/two-seater chair used two broken utility chairs which I found in the skip. I was fortunate to find two chairs of similar height and size to join together

Why not have a go at creating your own hybrid? Sketch out your ideas and plan carefully before you start. As my father (and technician!) always says, 'Measure twice, cut once!'

and finally...

I hope *Mixed Media and Found Materials* contains much exciting and useful guidance and that you have been inspired and motivated for your own projects.

The ideas in this book are merely starting points to be developed through your own particular imagination and creative energy. It's important to remember that when using found materials no outcome will ever be the same, and that's the beauty of it.

A friend said to me, 'Won't writing a book give all your ideas away?' My response was that as a creative person your ideas constantly evolve and develop, and I have a million ideas which I'm dying to experiment with. Every one idea I have may inspire 100 different ideas in other people. This is the brilliance of sharing creativity, and working with found materials – no two designs will ever be the same.

Having written this book, I too have been inspired and enthused to pursue new ideas and experiment with new concepts. I am currently involved in working with manufacturers and preparing exhibitions and trade fairs, and also collaborating with other designers who use found and recycled materials.

Keep trying out new ideas and playing around with found materials – the key words are 'keep experimenting'. The possibilities when working with mixed media and found textiles are endless.

Happy hunting!

suppliers & sources

Craftwise Ltd
5 Merrion Way
Merrion Centre
Leeds
LS2 8DB
www.craftwiseuk.com
Tel: 0113 2930636

Dylon International Ltd
Knowles House
Cromwell Road
Redhill
RH1 1RT
Email: info@dylon.co.uk
www.dylon.co.uk
Tel: 01737 742020

efabrics (Fabrics and haberdashery)
Chawla's
269 Bath Road
Hounslow
Middx
TW3 3DA
www.efabrics.co.uk
Tel: 0208 5722902

Fibrecrafts
Old Portsmouth Road
Peasmarsh
Guildford
Surrey
GU3 1LZ
www.fibrecrafts.com
Tel: 01483 565800

Groves and Bank material suppliers
Email: j.supple@groves-banks.com
Tel: 01844 258110

Lazertran™
www.lazertran.com
mic@lazertran.com
Tel: 01545 571149

Masons (Needlecraft)
Masons
22 Bath Street
Abingdon
Oxon
OX14 3QH
www.masonsneedlecraft.co.uk
Email: sales@masonsneedlecraft.co.uk
Tel: 01235 520107

A.W. Midgley and Son Ltd (Leather suppliers)
13 Cheddar Business Park
Wedmore Rd
Cheddar
Somerset
BS27 3EB
www.awmidgley.co.uk
Tel: 01943 741741

The Paper Shed (Paper-making equipment)
c/o Fibrecrafts
Old Portsmouth Road
Peasmarsh
Guildford
Surrey
GU3 1LZ
www.papershed.com
Tel: 01483 565800

Wood Veneer UK
www.woodveneeruk.co.uk

Pfaff Sewing Machines
Sewing and Repair Centre
126 Park View
Whitley Bay
Tyne & Wear
NE26 3QN
www.pfaffmachines.co.uk
Email:
salesenquires@pfaffmachines.co.uk
Tel: 0191 2525825

The Upholstery Shop
Bonners Ltd
35 Upper Wickham Lane
Welling
Kent DA16 3AB
www.upholsteryshop.co.uk
Tel: 0208 3011777

Whaleys Ltd
Harris Court
Great Horton
Bradford
West Yorkshire
BD7 4EQ
www.whaleys-bradford.ltd.uk
Email: info@whaleysltd.co.uk
Tel: 01274 576718

Salvage and junk shops

To find out where your local
car-boot sale is, see
www.carbootjunction.com

To find out where your local
jumble sale is, see
www.britinfo.net/events/uk-car-boot-
sales

These are some shops, local to me, that I
find useful:

Bamfords Auctioneers and Valuers Ltd
The Derby Auction House
Chequers Road
off Pentagon Island
Derby
DE21 6EN
Tel: 01332 210000
www.bamfords-auctions.co.uk

The Cattle Market car-boot sale, Derby

The Derbyshire Irondale Salvage Co.
19 Bridgeport Rd

Chaddesden
DE21 6WA
Tel: 01332 673000

Flourish Farm Antiques
Flourish Farm
Spondon Rd
Dale Abbey
Ilkeston
DE7 4PQ
www.flourishantiques.com
Tel: 01332 667820

Good Old Days
6 Flood St
Oakbrook
DE72 3RF
Tel: 01332 544244

Sue Ryder Shop
Nettlebed sales
Tel: 01491 641070
Email:
fundraising.nettlebed@suerydercare.org

Scrapstores

Orinoco Scrapstore
Bullingdon Community Centre
Peat Moors
Headington
Oxford
OX3 7HS
www.oxorinoco.org
Tel: 01865 761113

Burseldon Scrapstore
Email:
southampton.scrapstore@virgin.net
www.southamptonscrapstore.org.uk.
Tel: 023 8040 2810

Hackney Scrap
137 Homerton
High Street
Hackney
London
E9 6AS
Email: childrensscrap@btconnect.com
www.childrensscrap.co.uk
Tel: 0208 9856290

National UK scrapstore directory

To find out where your local
scrapstore is, see
www.childrensscrapstore.co.uk

Useful websites

www.textileonline.com
*Excellent site for information, current facts
and recommended books.*

www.wasteonline.org.uk

www.freecycle.org
*Network to promote waste reduction and
help save landscapes from being taken
over by landfill.*

www.wastebook.org
*Free guide to recycling and sustainable
waste management.*

index